Blockchain:

A 60-minute Guide to Blockchain Technology

By Gary Bukowski

Table of Contents

Introduction

Congratulations on downloading *Blockchain: A 60-minute Guide to Blockchain Technology* and thank you for doing so. Blockchain is a database that is truly on the cutting edge of technology at the moment. So much so that its true potential has not even come close to be discovered. Nevertheless, analysts of all types are already declaring it the most important technology since the Internet itself. While if you are not already familiar with Blockchain these claims might sound excessive, you will soon learn the reasons that Blockchain is likely to change the world in your lifetime.

The following chapters will discuss the ins and outs of Blockchain so that you can move forward with a clear understanding of the technology and how to possibly put it to use for your business. First, you will learn all about the beginnings of Blockchain and how it is tied to the history of Bitcoin. Next you will learn all about the inner workings of Blockchain that make it so useful as a decentralized database. From there you will learn about the reasons you might want to put Blockchain to use for your database needs as well as the reasons why it might not be right for you, right now. From there you will learn about many of the mistakes that users frequently make when implementing it so that you can avoid them yourself. Finally, you will learn how to create your own smart contracts and utilize Blockchain to its full potential.

There are plenty of books on this subject on the market, thanks again for choosing this one! Every effort was made to ensure it is full of as much useful information as possible, please enjoy!

Chapter 1

Blockchain History

If you have heard people using the term Blockchain recently but haven't been able to figure out exactly what it is they are talking about, there is a good reason for your confusion. While the term Blockchain has only been around for less than a decade, it has already come to mean several different things depending on the context it is used in. When it comes up in conversation, Blockchain typically is related to cryptocurrencies as a general concept, related to Bitcoin in particular or something having to do with smart contracts.

While the usage, and especially the proper usage, is bound to vary, there are several different things that all Blockchain conversations are bound to have in common. First and foremost, it is important to understand that Blockchains are a means for storing data, which is typically financial in nature, though not always, and its most important feature is that it is completely decentralized. Each new block in a chain contains all the data that the previous blocks do, along with new information based on the specifics surrounding that block. Once added, the new information filters back through all the other blocks as well.

Besides containing any new information along with all the other relevant information from the chain, each block also comes with a timestamp that makes note of when it was accessed while also helping the system to determine its correct spot in the chain as a whole. This, combined with its habit of automatically replicating itself, means that a Blockchain can work properly and catalogue data without the help of a server or any type of centralized authority that tells it how to track and store the data.

One Blockchain could potentially have thousands upon thousands of individual data nodes that could be spread out around the country or even around the world. Each of these nodes then communicates with the other nodes and forms a consensus when it comes to what the true version of the data they contain really is.

Regardless of their created purpose, all Blockchain users fall into one of two main types. These are individuals with write access and those with read-only access. While more traditional databases need to tightly control their access qualifications, Blockchain's decentralized nature means that changing the data it contains is a very costly and time-consuming proposition so access can be controlled less stringently. The details of Blockchain security will be discussed in detail in a later chapter.

It all started with Bitcoin: Bitcoin is already being hailed as one of the most important technologies to come out of the twenty-first century. As with all great inventions it had extremely humble beginnings. Blockchain began as a theory that was floating around on a peer-to-peer message board by a user by the name of Satoshi Nakamoto. Now this person was never properly identified which has led some people to believe that several different individuals shared use of the name. Nakamoto first hypothesized about a peer-to-peer online based currency that could exist without financial institutional backing in the mid-2000s.

From there, the Nakamoto persona presented a treatise on the idea called *Bitcoin: A P2P Electronic Cash System* along with the opensource code for what would ultimately become Bitcoin. As more and more people started to work with the source code, the Nakamoto name dropped out of the scene and was never heard from again after the 2010.

As one would not exist without the other, a little more detail regarding Bitcoin is required. A Bitcoin is a type of currency that is solely found online, with no real-world counterpart. Those who use Bitcoins can trade them for goods and services just as if they were a physical currency. These days, Bitcoin users can use them practically anywhere that other forms of payment are accepted, and it all happens without any type of centralized oversight.

Where Blockchain comes into the equation is that each Blockchain transaction is tracked and recorded in the same database that has been in use since the first Bitcoin transaction was recorded. As such, if you were so inclined you could go out and start your own Bitcoin node and you would download all of the information on every transaction.

When a new transaction occurs, it is checked for authenticity and accuracy by a private individual, known as a Bitcoin miner. This individual then makes use of the Bitcoin Blockchain and verifies the new information that is stored in a specific block to ensure it aligns with all of the previous blocks. For their effort, the miner then receives a fraction of a total Bitcoin to compensate them for their work. This process of unbiased third-party verification is a key component of what makes a decentralized database possible.

While a fraction of a Bitcoin might not sound like much, a single Bitcoin is currently worth more than $2,000. The value of a Bitcoin fluctuates based on the total number of other coins on the market as well as the global exchange rate as a whole, in just the way that more traditional currencies work. The Nakamoto alias formed the first block in the chain by gifting 50 Bitcoins to another user and then verifying the transaction. The first Bitcoin transaction occurred when someone used 10,000 of them to order a pizza in 2009 placing their original value at around .002 cents each.

Once the code hit the Internet, it was continuously improved upon until 2014 when users discovered that entire programs could be placed inside a single block. This led to the creation of smart contracts and an expansion for Blockchain into other types of data storage outside of the financial realm. A smart contract is a type of program that is capable of triggering once a set if/then statement has occurred within the Blockchain, which then moves funds from one location to another.

2016 then marked another big advancement for Blockchain technology, as it was when Ethereum, another cryptocurrency, made a big splash in the public consciousness. It has made the creation of smart contracts easier than ever before which have lead some people to declare that its code is the basis for what is known as Blockchain 2.0. Currently, Russia is utilizing this code to construct a means to combat copyright infringement, which makes Russia the first country to consider using Blockchain on a massive scale.

Decentralized and centralized databases: When it comes to the differences between Blockchain and more standard databases, the biggest difference is where the relevant data is physically stored. With traditional databases, servers and their relevant nodes are split up throughout a building or possibly a few square miles, though the distance is typically minimized as much as possible in order to improve retrieval speeds.

Blockchain nodes, on the other hand, can be literally anywhere which means that they are going to deal with a good deal more latency. While this isn't the best solution for those who need to store reams of data, it is great for those who are looking to store data outside of traditional confines and make sure that what is there is completely tamperproof. This is at the heart of what makes Blockchain so potentially disruptive to the status quo, it could potentially change the way the entire financial sector handles data collection and storage. Simply put, Blockchain is already on its way to revolutionize currency transactions the way the Internet changed the way information is transmitted.

Chapter 2

Breaking Down a Blockchain

Uncrackable cryptography: While the fact that each block in a Blockchain has the ability to replicate itself each time a new node comes online is certainly novel, it wouldn't be nearly as useful if that data wasn't both easy to see and difficult to tamper with without the proper clearance. Luckily, it is extremely easy to allow users to have read-only access to the data without worrying about them finding a backdoor solution that allows them to have write access as well. Additionally, the facet of Blockchain that makes it so secure isn't some code or other security measure that was created for this purpose, it is a key part of its very fabric.

Due to the fact that a Blockchain is completely decentralized, it needs a practical way to ensure that the information it contains is going to remain the same across every node in the network, even if one or more of the nodes goes offline for an extended period of time. In order to ensure that this is the case, each time a node connects to the system it automatically checks to ensure that any new information it acquires is the same as the data that currently exists on more than fifty percent of all the nodes that are part of the system. Incompatible data is then expunged from the system and replaced with the data supported by the status quo.

This means that in order for someone to change the data in the system, for example, trying to use the same Bitcoins to pay for two separate transactions, they would need to generate a false Blockchain showing the coins were not used for the initial transaction and then transmit that information to fifty-one percent of all of the Bitcoin nodes in the world. Doing so would be extremely time consuming and require a massive amount of energy, costing far more than such a ploy would ever be worth.

Ease of travel model: Information that is stored in the Blockchain comes in two primary types, the data related to relevant transaction and the information that is adjacent to this information which makes it easier for the chain to determine which blocks go where. The transaction data is what accounts for most of the space and is passed from node to node for verification purposes through what is known as the best-effort model. This means it moves from node to node based on which nodes would be easiest for it to move to next based on its current location which means it doesn't require a guiding hand to tell it what to do. When new data is found on any relevant node it is then verified as accurate before a new block is created around it, which is where third-party compensation and verification come into play.

Public and private options: While one of Blockchain's most important features is that so many people can look but not touch, that doesn't mean every chain has to be public. In fact, when a new chain is created you have the ability to limit its visibility however you deem fit. Private Blockchains are always going to have fewer costs than their public alternatives because they have to be much more complicated in order to discourage fraud. Additionally, they require additional steps when it comes to ensuring that each interaction is verified and validated in order to retain a semblance of order as well. These concerns are less important for private Blockchains as, in theory, each person who gains access has already been vetted and those with access can then validate new transactions for the benefit of the group as a whole.

Back to the Bitcoin example, if a person is interested in starting a Bitcoin node, the first thing they need to do is to download the Bitcoin source file which is known as the Bitcoin Core. This will allow them to verify transaction, and make a profit in the process. Once they verify the transaction they are then added to new blocks in the chain that is stored on their node, which is then further verified across the network before it becomes part of the official. If they were running a private Blockchain then none of this would be required as they would need clearance to access the chain in the first place. Secondary security measures are then left up to the creator's discretion.

Show your work: When a new transaction is verified by a node, it is first compared to all the other transactions stored on that node before being placed in the right place in the overall timeline. After this is completely the chain then inherently understands where the block falls in the chain as a whole. Beyond this, each block also contains what is known as a proof of work system which explains to the chain that it was created by the appropriate systems instead of some outside intruder. This proof of work contains a fair amount of complex mathematical computations, which require a decent amount of computational power to complete. It also scales based on the number of transactions which are being added in a single go which is what makes a new, fraudulent, chain so difficult to reproduce.

Hashes: Blockchain security is multifaceted which means that even assuming a third party could gain unauthorized access to a Blockchain they wouldn't be able to automatically gain access to all of the information that the Blockchain contains. Instead, they would be able to see a type of data known as fixed length outputs, which is akin to the unique fingerprint for each transaction. Changing even a single digit of this information can lead to massive, and unpredictable, results. The most commonly used form of this data is known as a hash function and hash function SHA-256 is the most commonly used. It takes the data provided by each new transaction and formats it in such a way that only another SHA-256 hash can decode it and make it readable in a more traditional fashion.

Each block is provided with a unique hash as soon as it is verified and added to the official chain. This basic hash is then altered even more based on where it is located in the chain and how its details affect the chain as a whole. If an alternative block is substituted and its hash details don't line up with those of its surrounding companions then when it reaches a new node the deviant block is nullified.

Various levels of automation: As a Blockchain is by its very nature decentralized, each node must have the ability to act autonomously for extended periods of time. Once it comes back in touch with the other nodes they all need to be able to seamlessly connect with one another and update their details based on what the out of touch node provides. When this occurs, the nodes that are physically closest to the transmitting node are automatically leaned on more heavily as their close proximity leads to their use via the best-effort definition. A final check then ensures that the new details contain nothing that is duplicated elsewhere or conflicts with the chain as a whole before this data is then officially accepted and disseminated throughout the entire network.

Merkle tree: The Merkle tree is a key part of the way in which data is stored on a Blockchain. While it is possible to build a Blockchain without utilizing this technology, those that are not nearly as efficient and it is more difficult to allow new users to access them. As previously mentioned, each block in a chain has multiple transactions stored inside. Each of these transactions was run through a hash function and provided their own unique has as part of the process. The pairs of hashes are then combined and then put through another hash function, creating even more unique hashes as a result.

This continues until the entire chain has a single unique hash which is known as the root hash. This root hash is referred to as a Merkle tree and it is the sum total of all of the various hashes that are a part of it. The Merkle tree is then used to secure the chain and alert each node if anything relating to any of the original hashes is altered in any way. Merkle trees then make it possible to run a decentralized node structure that is responsible for much of Blockchain's easy mutability. They are functionality matrices that focus on efficiency and utilizing complexity in the most efficient way possible. They make it possible for finances to be compacted into information that can then be parsed by uses as quickly and easily as possible.

Each Merkle tree has branches that split off from the root in factors of two. As such, each node has at least two branches as a means of distributing data verification as easily as possible. They can also be used to encode many different files that are smaller than the original file. They allow the same piece of information to exist in multiple places at once without having to worry about corruption should the two no longer agree.

Chapter 3

Deciding If Blockchain is Right for You

If all of this sounds as though it will meet your data storage needs and you feel as though you would like to experiment with Blockchain for your own purposes it is important to consider a few additional things before you go and construct your own Blockchain.

Understand who will have access to the data: When it comes to centralized databases, anyone with access to the database has their activities stored in case a review is required at a later date. If you need to give lots of users read-only access to your data and don't want to worry about having to limit them from write access then a Blockchain can easily streamline this process. You can set the Blockchain to be viewable in a non-hash format and still log access in a more traditional way if it is required.

Writeable data: Your average user database is typically protected via a mix of usernames and passwords along with several levels of restricted access. Even more security measures can then be implemented to prevent high-level data from being accessed when it shouldn't. All of this is still less than the standard Blockchain security protocols which always makes it perfectly clear who created which blocks and the time and place they did so.

This ensures that each transaction is always completed with the full knowledge of the creator who can then confirm and sign off on the transaction assuming the individuals are not adding information directly from a node. This signature is then further confirmed before the block is added to the chain. Even if a username and password combination are not required in order for users to have access (not recommended) the chain will still automatically log the IP address of any user who creates new blocks.

Consider how often you will need to change stored information: If you are going to need to change the information that has already been added to the chain on a regular basis then you may want to reconsider using Blockchain. This is because it is more difficult to change data than it is with a more traditional database. In a standard database, someone with the right level of access can simply go in and change the data that needs to be changed. In a Blockchain database, however, the data needs to be changed across fifty-one percent of the active nodes in order for the chain to not consider it an aberration. What's more, these changes will all need to be made at the same time, or the nodes will need to be taken offline so that the Blockchain registers all of the changes at once. Either way, this process tends to be both cumbersome and time consuming.

Backing up data: When using a standard database, backing up files is never without risk as it is always possible for the backup to become corrupted or for it not to contain the right information. All of these potential issues are rendered moot when using a Blockchain database, however, as the information is automatically stored across all of the connected nodes and updated as new information is added.

This makes the traditional backup system completely irrelevant as even if a node is completely corrupted then all of the data is going to be there waiting for it once you get things back up and running. Depending on the scope of your data usage and how often you are currently creating backups, running a Blockchain database might actually be cheaper than your current system, even when the added costs of running a distributed network are taken into account.

Legal challenges: Blockchain data moves between nodes without any concern for physical boundaries. As such, if you are dealing with highly confidential information that can't leave a physical boundary then you will need to either ensure all of your nodes are within that space or you will need to keep certain nodes offline in most instances. Both of these options negate many of the benefits of decentralized databases which means you might be better off sticking with a conventional setup.

Interconnectivity: If the business you are in necessitates frequent exchanges of database information with other organizations for set periods of time then you will likely find that a decentralized database is a welcome change from the status quo. Blockchain makes it easy to connect disparate Blockchains together for a set amount of time to ensure interoperability at previously unheard-of levels. If you create this type of interaction it is important to always take the appropriate precautions to ensure the other party can look but only touch when appropriate.

Types of data: Before you make plans for a new Blockchain database it is important to understand the type of data that you are going to be storing to ensure it works well with the infrastructure. The best type of data to store in blocks is that which is relatively small and fairly simple as sending blocks that are stuffed with several gigabytes of data to distant nodes is sure to be a cumbersome and difficult process. Unless some other aspect of Blockchain makes this worth the effort, and remember it will be happening every time new information is added, then you may want to stick with a centralized database until Internet speeds improve.

Data validation: The most continuous cost of running a decentralized database comes from the cost of validating each transaction that takes place amongst all of your nodes. To understand how much this upkeep is going to cost you, it is important to consider the data that is going to be placed into each block and how frequently new blocks are going to be created each month. The lower either of these numbers are, the less the costs will be but they will still need to be paid either by the creator of the database or by the community who will then need to be compensated for the time they put in as well as the energy costs they accrue.

The costs will ultimately be determined by how popular the Blockchain is and how much use on a daily basis it sees. If you run a public Blockchain then you will be able to count on individuals who can validate in return for incentives, and if your chain is private then some of these costs can be deferred to other members. Each individual who validates adds extra costs but also ensures that any potential errors are spotted and corrected as quickly as possible.

Getting started

If, after working your way through these considerations you still believe that switching to a Blockchain database makes sense, the next thing you will want to do is determine your plan when it comes to how you want Blockchain to work for you. If you are looking to add a Blockchain to an existing business then you will want to consider the ways in which Blockchain and smart contracts can help your company react in a more dynamic fashion in the marketplace in ways that will help you outmaneuver your competition. It is best to start when it comes to the automation of tasks that will help decrease costs, improve efficiency and increase revenue.

What's more, you are going to want to consider how the adoption of Blockchain technology at large is going to disrupt the standard operating procedures of the business you are in. Understanding these future disruptions will make it easier for you to future proof your business now, so that you will have less to worry about as adoption rates increase. Doing so will not only make you a leader when it comes to emerging trends in your field, it will increase your competitive standing compared to other businesses in your market and in the eyes of your target audience. After all, the earlier you can determine what's coming down the pipeline, the easier it will be to prepare for its results.

On the other hand, if you find yourself with a startup idea that can utilize Blockchain to enhance your odds of gaining market share in a crowded market then the first thing you are going to want to do is to start getting as much hands-on experience with Blockchain as you can manage. This means you are going to want to get involved anywhere and everywhere that is currently using Blockchain so you can really get your hands dirty. This will ensure that when the technology really hits the mainstream you will be head of the curve. Additionally, through your involvement you can strive to enhance the overall acceptance of the new technology as quickly as possible.

Chapter 4

Blockchain Disadvantages

Before you go ahead and pull the trigger on your new Blockchain database you will want to be aware of certain peculiarities of the system along with drawbacks that might make the technology more trouble than its worth for the time being.

Costs: While there is plenty about Blockchain that streamlines the gathering and transmission of data, this does not extend to its costs or the ease with which it can be operated. What's more, these are not issues that are likely to improve anytime soon as they are inherent in the distributed nature of the network, which leads to most of the system's strengths. Each node that you add to the system is going to add to the network's overall security, but also to its costs in equal measure. Additionally, these costs tend to add up at the rate of one to one as the costs for setting up ten nodes are going to be roughly ten times that of setting up a single node with little breaks for bulk along the way.

Due to the fact that costs and demand do not scale in a beneficial, starting a Blockchain database is not going to be possible for many companies, especially those with a fully functioning centralized database already up and running. While extra costs are going to vary based on specifics, a good rule of thumb when it comes to anticipating them is that it takes the same amount of power to confirm a single Bitcoin transaction as the average household uses in 36 hours. While the Bitcoin Blockchain is the largest currently in existence, the cost is only ever going to increase which is something to keep in mind when considering your own Blockchain as well.

Minimizing the efficacy of data mining: While consumers might appreciate the fact that it is difficult for companies to mine data from a Blockchain, this could easily be a deal breaker for you if your business regularly borrows details from transaction data that would be moved to the Blockchain under the new system. The inherent level of anonymity that each transaction is granted makes it largely impossible to track the habits of individual users with currently available technology. What's more, until this issue is solved, it will seriously harm Blockchain's ability to gain mass acceptance, as major corporations need to be on the bandwagon, not in the way.

Extra complications: While the interactions that a single user will have with your Blockchain are typically going to be relatively straightforward, maintenance of the Blockchain itself can be quite complicated and time-consuming to boot thanks to its distributed nature. This means that if you are planning on switching your database over from a centralized to a decentralized version you will need to account for all the extra man-hours and costs that this will require.

Additionally, you will need to plan for the fact that a Blockchain database is typically much more complicated than a centralized database, even if the overall information that is being stored is the same. This means that if you are looking for additional security or backup protection, and nothing else, then there are likely going to be easier and cheaper means of acquiring what it is you are looking for. If Blockchain is ever going to reach a level of mass acceptance then creating and maintaining them is going to need to be streamlined significantly.

Not truly safe: While the means for hacking a Blockchain currently almost certainly exceed the benefits at the moment, as more and more businesses get on board then this is almost certainly not going to be the case forever. It requires a vast amount of computational power, but once the right information is up for grabs, this will become a reasonable expenditure for someone with questionable morals and the right desires. While it is functionally impossible to generate the power to recreate a majority of a Blockchain as of 2017, it won't remain this way forever.

Pro big business: While Blockchain technology is currently in the hands of the fringes of the business world, it is bound to catch on with major corporations sooner or later. What's more, these types of organizations have the most to gain from using the technology and also have the resources to implement it with the fewest issues. They control the access to the types of infrastructure and resources that make the transition from centralized to decentralized processes, not only feasible but cost effective as well.

Each new technology always follows the same pattern of adoption. First, the fringes catch on to a great new thing and proselytize its virtues. The technology then rises to a greater degree of prominence, taking a handful of small businesses with it into the limelight. The rest are then crushed as existing players in every marketplace adopt and adapt to the new technology. This has happened with every new technology since the Industrial Revolution and it is unrealistic to expect Blockchain to be any different. This isn't necessarily a downside to Blockchain as a useful tool, just something that needs to be kept in mind as its implementation becomes more commonplace.

New security concerns: While pretty much anyone can purchase the right equipment and start verifying Bitcoin transactions, when the Blockchain is put to use in corporate scenarios this will no longer be the case. Those who are hired expressly to verify transactions will have a level of access that is unprecedented when it comes to being able to modify data that they have access to. The amount of power that these individuals will have will almost certainly require a new level of security monitoring to be put in place in order to prevent the wrong sort of individuals from having access to this power. This, in turn, means additional costs and security measures, at the very least.

Too efficient: While many in the financial sector can be heard expounding on the virtues of Blockchain as a game changer when it comes to trading securities, the fact of the matter is that the major players in each market like the pace at which things currently move. Real time settlements are different than same day settlements as they make it easier for the buyer to receive the shares almost instantly. This, in turn is bad for sellers who in often case don't have enough liquidity to give up the shares right away without cutting into their profits elsewhere.

The fact of the matter is that you can make real-time exchanges in many countries and in the United States as well, but this will always be the exception to the rule until enough about the markets change that this type of transaction benefits the wealthy in a way that makes them campaign for a change to the status quo.

It can't grow too quickly: While a mass and sudden adoption of Blockchain technology might sound good in theory, in practice a slow and steady increase is going to be better for everyone in the long term. This is the case due to the fact that the version of Blockchain that is going to stick around the longest is going to be the one that gains the widest acceptance among the masses. If the current version of Blockchain was "the one" then it is unlikely that many currently existing bugs would ever be worked out, or at least would be conquered at a much slower rate overall. If the technology catches on before it has reached an optimized state then these problems become much more difficult to fix as Blockchain is an open source technology which means that there is no centralized authority who can profit from making changes to the systems that major corporations have sunk money into interfacing with.

This means that Blockchain as a whole is better off moving along at an acceptance rate that is measured enough to give freelance programmers the time they need to develop the best version of the technology they can. If this sounds unlikely, consider the vast adoption rates of Windows XP and how long business around the world kept working on software that was more than a decade old compared with how quickly people update to the latest version of their phone's OS once it has been made available. The acceptance of Blockchain technology is a marathon, not a sprint, slow and steady wins the race.

Chapter 5

Mistakes to Avoid

While there are plenty of valid reasons to go about implementing your own Blockchain, the previous chapter showed why they might not be for everyone, at least not yet. For those to whom Blockchain seems to be the answer to their current problems, it is important to keep in mind that there is still plenty that can go wrong when it comes to putting your new database into place in such a way that the process proceeds as smoothly as possible. Keeping the following implementation mistakes in mind will make it much easier to avoid many of the common pitfalls the unaware stumble into when it comes to making their Blockchain dreams a reality.

Considering a Blockchain the answer to everything: There is plenty of hype these days surrounding Blockchain, which means the uninitiated can be forgiven for letting their expectations get away from them. Blockchain does have its limits, however, and you would do well to remember them if you want to implement one in the best way possible.

As such, when it comes to implementation you are going to want to consider exactly what you are going to need your Blockchain to do in order to keep it from acting like just another database except that it is more expensive to run. This is especially true when it comes to the amount of data that you will be storing as all of it is going to need to be copied across every node you set up, both initially and through the entire lifetime of the database as well. While a few extra gigs of data, now and then, may not seem like much in theory in practice however it will be noticeable, especially if the distance between nodes is significant.

For example, Bitcoin's Blockchain is currently only around 60 gigs and it is the largest Blockchain currently in existence by far. The lesson here is that the most effective Blockchain databases are either those that keep things as compact as possible or those that only require portions of their information to be accessed on a regular basis.

Additionally, you are going to want to keep in mind that while Blockchain databases naturally have fail safes when it comes to mitigating the effects of user error, they are no more immune to the phenomena than any other database would be. In fact, their largely obfuscated nature actually makes them more prone to user error in many ways, especially as individual blocks are typically only identifiable via their hash identifier, which can easily lead to confusion. While this will become less of an issue as the technology becomes more mainstream, it is important to keep in mind that there is more to starting a Blockchain than simply getting it up and running correctly.

Expecting a simple solution: If you hope to see your transition to a decentralized database all the way through, it is vital that you create a roadmap ahead of time to guarantee you understand all the steps you will need to follow in order to get it up and running. In order to ensure this map is accurate, it is important that you fully understand Blockchain up front along with all of its potential. While this book is a great first step in that direction, it is only that, which means additional work on your end will be required in order to understand it completely. If you truly want to balance out the cost versus the results then a deeper and more thorough understanding of the underlying specifics of the technology is required.

To make sure you are moving in the right direction it is important that you start off with an idea of what your database is going to be used for primarily as well as what any secondary responsibilities it is going to have. This will then allow you to consider which Blockchain creation tools you are going to need to help allow the process to proceed as smoothly as possible. Remember, just because the technology isn't mainstream yet, doesn't mean there isn't plenty of software out there that can make the process much easier for you to complete, all you need to do is to search for it. Rushing through this step can only hurt you in the long run and should be avoided at all costs.

Expecting it to be a quick process: Right from the start, it is important to give yourself all the time you will need to get your Blockchain database up and running as being impatient and rushing through the process will only lead to additional problems. The steps for doing so can often be very precise and not doing things in just the right way, or not testing your creation before it goes live are surefire ways to guarantee that you will need to repeat the process again. The best way to prevent this is to generously pad the timeframe for building the database, especially if you feel as though you are going to need to get input from multiple sources throughout the project.

Expecting too much from fail-safes: Blockchain's security is currently top of the line, but this doesn't mean that you are going to want to provide everyone who asks with access to your creation. While private Blockchains are going to exist in an environment that is much more controlled than their public counterparts, the fact of the matter is that if too many people have access to a newly created database too soon, especially if they have not been trained fully, then the Blockchain can collapse under the weight of too much inaccurate information as it won't have a valid information base to pull from when it comes to accurately determining the errors.

Additionally, it is important to keep in mind that the security that surrounds the heart of your Blockchain needs to be as strong as any that would be placed in a traditional database. Your access key to the Blockchain's inner workings will only be generated a single time and if you lose it then you lose control of the Blockchain with no way to get it back besides starting from scratch. Keep this in mind and control the access key accordingly.

Expecting too much from smart contracts: A smart contract is a program that can be added to a specific block of a Blockchain to allow the chain to do more than simply compile existing information. With the code, and its related parameters, in place, it can then react to certain stimuli in set ways once various actions have occurred. The contract is triggered by a set event, such as moving funds between two specific accounts once a certain amount is reached in the donor account. If someone else tries to alter these specifics then the Blockchain fail safes will kick in and prevent the change from occurring. The nature of a Blockchain means that the data will continue even if the system partially fails in one or more nodes.

Despite the name, smart contracts and real contracts have little in common. Smart contracts can automate the processes that are outlined in a traditional contract but they are not legally enforceable on their own. For example, a smart contract could be set up to automatically pay your car payment each month, and even shut down the operation of your vehicle if it was Internet enabled and the payment wasn't made, but it cannot force you to make the payment in question.

Instead, smart contracts really shine when it comes to automating the if/then statements found in a traditional contract as long as it contains hard facts that the smart contract can verify before getting to work. It is also important to point out that smart contracts are not Ricardian contracts, which are used primarily to determine liability. A smart contract will only activate after liability in one way or another, has already been proven. The best way to think of a smart contract is as though it were a switch that can be set to on or off with no opinion or way to determine which is the more ideal state.

Despite their relatively limited range, the variety of situations where a smart contract can come in handy is already quite large and growing every day. The parameters don't even need to exist solely within the Blockchain as long as extra steps are taken to give it access to the third-party source. Soon, any action that has clear indicators will realistically be able to be control by the Blockchain as long as the operating device is connected to the Internet.

Chapter 6

Utilizing Smart Contracts

If you are interested in proceeding with your own Blockchain and creating your own smart contracts then you are going to want to work with the Ethereum platform. As previously mentioned, the Ethereum platform has made the creation of smart contracts much easier than it was previously and it is still considered the hands-down leader in that space. As with Bitcoin, the Ethereum currency, called ether, is a cryptocurrency, though unlike Bitcoin, it focuses on giving those looking to pay for services an easy an anonymous way of doing so. It can also be used to run a number of applications that have been created to specifically run on its platform. As of 2017, 1 ether is currently worth about $200.

One of Ethereum's most unique aspects is that it boasts the ability to host decentralized applications along with databases. Each application can then link directly to a Blockchain and connect to any related smart contracts without the user having to log into an actual node in order to do so. As such, you do not even need to run your own node to take full advantage of the Ethereum platform though it is recommended that you do so as it is great practice and it makes testing smart contracts a much easier process.

When it comes to the actual creation of smart contracts the best way to currently go about doing so is via the Solidity programing language, which is based off JavaScript. You are also going to want to download LLL, an offshoot of Lisp and always create your files using the .se or .sol extension. Solidity will be a natural fit for those who have previously used either Serpent or Python.

Once you are ready to compile contracts, the best way to go about doing so is with the SOLC C++ compiler. If that won't work for you, then Cosmo is a complier that is browser based and is typically considered the natural alternative. The following step-by-step instructions will assume that you are utilizing the SOLC complier though most of the instructions will apply to Cosmo as well. After the compiling step has been finished, the next thing you will need to do is to download the API Web3.ja in order to interact with the contracts you create through the Ethereum application.

Frameworks

If you don't like the idea of building your own framework, there are plenty of free ready-made options to choose from. What follows is a list of the best currently on the market.

Truffle: Truffle is a useful framework if you are looking to automate as much of the creation process as you possibly can. It automatically completes a large number of standard programming steps that need to be performed on a regular basis. With these out of the way you will then have more time to focus on creating the best code possible through an increased focus on testing, compiling changes and deploying your smart contract. Bundled with Truffle, Embark makes the streamline process even easier.

Meteor: Meteor is a stack that works with web3.js which makes working with Blockchain even easier. Meteor is an increasingly popular framework and was discussed heavily at the last Ethereum Development conference.

API: The majority of the Ethereum based applications these days come from BlockApps.net. This site makes it easy to discover APIs that make it easy to mimic Ethereum nodes which, in turn, makes it easier to interact with smart contracts on the go. MetaMask is a popular API that provides access to a complete suite of Ethereum tools from any web browser. LightWallet is a more in-depth API that is somewhat more complicated as well. It is the API that is used most frequently by professional Blockchain developers.

Install Geth

Get started: In order to build your own Blockchain, the first thing that you will need to do is to install the Ethereum interface that all nodes and applications make use of which is called Geth. Geth can be installed from the command line via this command: bash<(curlhttps://install-geth.ethereum.org). This will prompt a dialogue box that will ask if you wish to install Geth before asking you what version of the Ethereum CLL you are running along with the operating system you are installing too.

Once this installation has finished, you will then be able to interact with the Geth interface, by and large, in the same ways that you can interact with the JavaScript environment as well as the console at the same time. Any console use is then automatically tracked to ensure you always pick up where you left off. With this done, you will then want to open the terminal tool to access the Geth console. With the program launched, the first thing you are going to need to do is to look for the greater than symbol in the lower right corner which is the indicator that everything is working properly. When you wish to quit you simply type exit and hit the enter key. You can also redirect inside Geth along with logging console outputs through the use of the gethconsole2>>geth.log command. If you need to locate the log it is available by entering the tailfgeth.log.

Test a smart contract

When creating a smart contract, it is crucial that all of your if/then statements work out properly and that there is absolutely no leeway when it comes to setting specific events that make the contract due what it was created to do. The simplest way to ensure that this is the case is through Truffle which will then automatically create the right type of framework the promises required for both Web3.js and JavaScript.

Transaction time test: It is important to keep your smart contract promises as simple as possible as it will be difficult for your Blockchain to verify in less than 10 seconds. In fact, this is still quite a fast time and is typically only possible via optimal testing conditions. This means the more promises that it needs to cross-reference, the longer the process is going to take.

When it comes time to actually test the contract the first thing you are going to want to do is to re-label the .js file to conference.js and change any other references as well. Once this is done you will want to open Truffle and run the test based on the root directory that the contract is located in.

To run this test properly you will need to open Pip, Solidty and SOLC, and be careful to separate the test library from the main library as well. You will then need to open the console window and create a new client node before using the Truffle deploy command and ensuring the contract is set to the standard init. This will allow the program to track any errors found in the code so you don't need to do it manually. This is also a good time to test the compilation process to prevent it from throwing up errors at the last minute.

Finish the contract

Once you have finished creating the contract in Solidity, you will need to compile it with the SOLC compiler. After this is finished you can then deploy it after you have signed a digital signature that certifies you as the creator of the content. You will then need to pay the fee in ether to get the contract up and running. After this has been completed you will then receive a unique URL which links to the contract and can be used to link the contract API with the API of your choice. Checking on the contract after this is a free option, though there are also additional things you can do for a small ether fee.

When you create a smart contract, it is a good idea to always include a variable that will make it easy for you to shut it down completely through the use of a suicide command. This is important as if anything goes wrong with the contract, any funds that it is holding will be stuck in limbo without the suicide command. Once the contract is destroyed any funds that it is holding will revert back to their previous accounts. Including this option up front is much easier than having to go back and add it in later.

Deploy the contract

After the contract is up and running it can then be deployed through the use of the Truffle console command truffle init, followed by the name of the directory you are deploying it into. After this has been completed you will be able to find the contract's new location by searching for its name with the extension .sol. Once you find the contract you are looking for you will want to open the configuration file for the app.json before adding the new contract into the space for new contract names.

Once this has been completed the last thing that you will need to do is open an Ethereum node in a separate console window and use the command run tesrpc. Assuming you have done everything else correctly you can then deploy the contract from Truffle with the deploy option that can be found in the root directory.

Conclusion

Thank you for making it through to the end of *Blockchain: A 60-minute Guide to Blockchain Technology*, let's hope it was informative and able to provide you with all of the tools you need to achieve your goals, whatever it is that they may be. Just because you've finished this book doesn't mean there is nothing left to learn on the topic, expanding your horizons is the only way to find the mastery you seek.

At the moment, Blockchains are largely prized for their ability to transmit financial data. This is all going to change, and likely sooner rather than later. Having read this book, you are now ready to get in on the ground floor when this change occurs. While real world examples of smart contracts are currently rather sparse, new uses for the technology are being discovered all the time. While smart contracts are currently in the hands of those in power, such as automatic deductions from your checking account, future innovations are sure to return that power to the people where it belongs. This will only happen, however, if the technology develops in the right way, which is where you come in.

Smart contract and Blockchain implementation is at a point where literally anything is possible. If you take the time to consider the optimal uses for this technology in the future, who knows what you can accomplish. If you aren't quite sure which direction you want to move in, don't worry, you still have plenty of time. You are still well ahead of the curve for the technology so there is no reason you need to feel as if you should rush. Take your time and consider all of the possible alternatives available to you and the right way to move forward will surely reveal itself. Remember, Blockchain and smart contract mastery is a marathon, not a sprint, slow and steady wins the race.

Finally, if you found this book useful in anyway, a review on Amazon is always appreciated!